KIM'S UNTOLD CHAPTERS

Truths, Trials, and Triumphs of an
Unforgettable Icon.

KATHERINE J. HARPER

DISCLAIMER

This book is based on the true experiences and journey of Kim, who wished for her story to be shared with the public.

This book is intended for informational and educational purposes only and should not be considered legal, medical, or professional advice. The author and publisher disclaim any liability for any loss or damage incurred as a result of the use of this book.

TABLE OF CONTENTS

INTRODUCTION

Can you believe it? Fresh out of high school, I was swept into the dazzling whirl of modeling. It was surreal, exciting, and everything moved at lightning speed. Then, I met Al B Sure. Our romance was a whirlwind—we fell deeply in love, got married young, and were blessed with our son, Quincy, who's grown into an incredible man.

But life had more in store for me. Al's introduction to Sean Combs would unknowingly pivot my life from a fairy tale to a psychological thriller. Sean, with his charming facade, seemed perfect, but beneath that charm lurked a different reality—one that I would come to fear and despise.

Despite the red flags, I turned a blind eye, lying to myself because the truth was too painful to admit. Now, I can no longer keep silent. The story of deceit, manipulation, and the quest for truth needs to be told—for my children, for myself, and for anyone who's ever found themselves ensnared by a wolf in sheep's clothing. It's time to expose Sean Combs."

HUMBLE BEGINNINGS: The Foundation of Strength

Born to Jake and Sarah L. Porter in the heart of Georgia, my early life was steeped in the warmth of community and the enduring spirit of the Peach State. Columbus High School, where I graduated in 1988, was my launchpad. I always had this inkling I was meant for something big—something beyond the familiar streets of my hometown.

A pivotal moment came during my sophomore year when my friend Tina threw down a challenge that would set the course of my future. "You won't make it here in Georgia," she said. Those words struck a chord. I knew then that to chase the stardom I dreamed of, I'd have to step beyond the comforts of home.

Life accelerated when I entered the entertainment industry. It was there I met Al. He was everything you'd imagine in a heartthrob—charismatic, captivating, and impossible not to fall for. Our romance was a whirlwind; soon, we were married and welcoming our son Quincy into the world. Despite our love, youth and reality clashed, and our marriage didn't last. However, our bond, sealed by Quincy, remained unbroken. Al, forever the phenomenal man and father, earned my eternal gratitude.

Then came Sean, a new chapter. Initially, he was just another face at the label, but his charm was relentless. As a single mom in one of the most exhilarating workplaces, life was exhilarating. Our relationship took off, blending personal joy with professional highs.

However, amidst the highs, there was a moment that tested my boundaries like never before. Sean's curiosity about new experiences brought us to an encounter that was both shocking and defining—it pushed me to a limit I hadn't anticipated and ultimately, it was a line I couldn't cross again. This experience, though uncomfortable, was a stark reminder of my own values and the boundaries I needed to maintain.

These stories of love, challenge, and self-discovery are not just recollections of past events; they are the pillars of my resilience and strength. From the encouraging words of a high school friend to the complex relationships that shaped my journey, each step was crucial in sculpting the person I am today.

SEAN KNEELS: A Pivotal Moment

That year, things with Sean seemed stable—few arguments, just the peculiarities of a man who was increasingly drawn to the mystical, if not outright bizarre. Sean's new fascination with Voodoo, casting spells and laying curses, was something out of a gothic novel, and I found it as intriguing as it was unsettling.

Despite the oddities, my desire to marry again as a single mother grew. However, Sean's career was skyrocketing. The success of Biggie and the signing of talents like Mary J. Blige only catapulted him further into the spotlight—a spotlight that, as I painfully discovered, included intimate encounters with Mary. His betrayal was a hard pill to swallow, yet in a complicated twist of emotions and desires, his proposition for a threesome with her led to an experience that was unexpectedly exhilarating. This encounter opened a new chapter of exploration and complexity in my life.

As time passed, Sean and I continued to invite others into our private moments, a practice that brought a strange sense of fulfillment. Yet nothing could prepare me for the day I found Sean and Al B Sure, my son Quincy's father, together in my home. The setup was innocuous enough: a casual sit-down that soon spiraled into an awkward revelation. Sean's suggestion that we all get together in a way we hadn't before left me stunned. The air thickened with tension, and Al's tentative agreement only added to the surreal nature of the moment.

The proposition was fraught with complications, not just for our relationships but for what it meant for Quincy, should things turn sour. Amid the shock and the underlying curiosity, the line between excitement and chaos blurred. The ensuing moments were too overwhelming, pushing me to a brink I hadn't anticipated. I fled, unable to process the rapid unraveling of boundaries.

This incident marked a pivotal moment in my journey, a stark confrontation with the limits of my adventures with Sean. It was a boundary crossed, a line redrawn in the complex map of my personal relationships. The echoes of that day lingered, a reminder of the intricate dance between passion and discretion, and how easily one could tip into the other.

As I wrestled with these revelations, I stumbled upon even more shocking truths about Sean—truths that would eventually reshape my understanding of who he was, and who I was in the wake of our shared history. The journey was far from over, and the vault of secrets I later discovered would only deepen the mystery and the challenges ahead.

LETTING GO: The Power of Forgiveness

F orgiveness isn't just a word; it's a journey, and often, a challenging one. That evening, when Sean arrived to see Quincy, something in me stirred. He brought flowers, his charm on full display, and there was Quincy, running to him with the pure love only a child can have, calling him, "Tiger." The simple, heartfelt exchange between them—"I miss you," "Me too, we'll hang out tomorrow"—softened the hardened layers of resentment I harbored.

Yet, here was the man who had deeply hurt me, not just emotionally but physically. His actions were inexcusable—the violent outbursts, the demands that pushed boundaries beyond comfort. And still, there he stood, the father figure Quincy adored. As Sean invited me out, promising a night just about fun, part of me wanted to believe in the possibility of change, of returning to those carefree days before everything went awry.

Sitting beside him, laughter filling the space between us, it felt like old times. But the arrival of the babysitter, and our departure, served as a reminder of the complexities of our relationship. The presence of Gene, the bodyguard with a visible gun, was jarring yet oddly reassuring. His polite demeanor, his respectful nod, offered a contrast to the tumultuous emotions swirling inside me.

Gene became a familiar face, a reminder that life goes on, and sometimes, in the most unexpected moments, we find pieces of ourselves we thought were lost. Forgiveness started to seem less like a concession and more like a gift I could give myself. It wasn't about condoning Sean's past actions or the pain he caused; it was about releasing the hold that bitterness had on my heart.

This night marked the beginning of my understanding of forgiveness. It was a recognition that holding onto the pain was a choice, and so was letting it go. As I slowly peeled back the layers of hurt, I found underneath not just the scars but also a resilience and a capacity for compassion I hadn't realized I possessed.

Through forgiveness, I began to reclaim my power, learning that forgiveness isn't just about the other person; it's profoundly about healing oneself. It's a path to freedom, a way to unshackle oneself from the chains of the past, and to embrace the potential for a new, more hopeful future.

This chapter of Kim's story explores the complex dance of forgiveness—how it intertwines with love, betrayal, and the ongoing quest for personal peace. It highlights the transformative power of letting go, not for the sake of the one who wronged us, but for our own sake, to live unfettered and whole.

SECOND CHANCES:
Redefining Paths

In life, second chances are not just about giving someone else another shot; sometimes, they're about allowing ourselves to see new possibilities, even when the path is fraught with challenges. My journey with Sean was a testament to this complex dance of choices and chances.

After a tumultuous period, Sean and I briefly lost touch, only to be unexpectedly reunited at a social event. Despite my attempts to maintain distance, his persistence wore down my defenses. "You look so amazing," he complimented, pulling at the threads of my resolve. His words, his gaze, they hinted at regret and a desire to rewrite our narrative. "I'm falling in love with you. Can we talk?" he pleaded. It was a pivotal moment; one where the past and its shadows loomed large, yet the possibility of a new beginning seemed within reach.

I agreed to dinner, a decision that marked the start of a year-and-a-half of what appeared to be normalcy. We enjoyed moments that mirrored the dreams of my youth, immersed in a world where Sean was making significant strides in his career with Bad Boy Records, signing artists like Craig Mack and The Notorious B.I.G. It felt like a rebirth of our relationship, a narrative punctuated by success and shared aspirations.

However, the veneer of normalcy cracked when Sean revisited past indiscretions, requesting to reenact a night that had previously pushed our boundaries too far. His plea, "Can you screw me one more time, please?" was a jarring echo of past mistakes. When he reacted violently to my refusal, the illusion shattered. It was a stark reminder that some cycles are hard to break, and the allure of second chances can sometimes lead us back to familiar pains.

Despite the altercation, the cycle of reconciliation reinitiated. Sean's gestures of remorse—flowers, gifts—were familiar overtures that tugged at the strings of my conflicted heart. When we met again, his plea, "I love you, I love your son. He's my son too... I don't know how to fix this, but I'll do anything. I'm sorry," resonated with a part of me still clinging to the hope of what could be.

In that moment, standing on the precipice of decision, I realized that second chances are not merely about forgiveness or reconciliation; they're about choosing paths that might lead to new horizons. As Sean walked away, my impulse to reconnect, despite everything, was a testament to the complex layers of human relationships—our vulnerabilities, our hopes, and our relentless pursuit of happiness, even in the face of past pains.

This chapter illustrates how Kim embraced second chances, not just with Sean, but in her own life's narrative, continually redefining her path and discovering new possibilities for growth and fulfillment. It's a reflection on the power of hope and the courage to pursue what could be, despite knowing what has been.

PAC: Legacy of a Legend

Tupac Shakur, or simply Pac, was more than just an icon in the world of hip-hop. He was a revolutionary spirit, a man who wore his heart on his sleeve, and someone whose presence in my life left an indelible mark. When I met Pac, I was already deep into my complicated relationship with Sean, and although things between Sean and me were unconventional, Pac brought a fresh perspective—a stark contrast to everything Sean represented.

At the time, Sean and I had an open relationship. To Sean, everything was a game—pushing boundaries, testing limits, and seeing how far his power could take him. Pac was different. He was a man of conviction, deeply passionate about his craft, his people, and his beliefs. The night Sean made an inappropriate advance toward Pac, it was a defining moment. Pac wasn't just angry about the disrespect aimed at him; he stood up for me in a way Sean never had. "Damn bro, you ain't gotta do the sister that way," Pac said, drawing a line that Sean couldn't see. In that moment, Pac showed me a different kind of respect, a respect I realized I had been missing in my relationship with Sean.

Sean, ever the instigator, kept pushing. His crude, competitive challenge to Pac, a man who had no interest in Sean's games, was the beginning of the end of any potential bond between them. Pac's refusal to engage in Sean's disrespectful behavior, and his subsequent exit, was one of the first times I witnessed the power of standing firm in your values. It was a moment that left me questioning everything I had accepted up until then.

Pac's refusal to be pulled into Sean's world of manipulation and control made me see him in a new light. He wasn't just a talented rapper; he was a man who knew his worth and wasn't afraid to walk away when something didn't align with his principles. For me, this was the start of understanding that second chances and new paths weren't just about trying again—they were about knowing when to walk away from the wrong situations.

In the months that followed, tension simmered between Pac and Sean. Every time they were in the same room, you could feel it—the unspoken anger, the bitterness of Sean's rejected advances, and Pac's silent refusal to play along. I was caught in the middle, torn between loyalty to Sean and admiration for Pac's unwavering stance. Then came "The Conversation"—the moment that shifted everything. Walking into Sean's office, I overheard the words that would haunt me forever. Sean, sitting across from Jimmy Henchman, gave the order, "Pac don't leave that studio alive."

It was a gut-wrenching moment. I realized then that Sean's power was more dangerous than I ever imagined. It was no longer just about games or infidelity—this was life and death. The man I once loved had crossed a line, one that could never be undone. And Pac, the man who had shown me what true respect and integrity looked like, became a target in a world that thrived on power and betrayal.

Pac's legacy in my life wasn't just about music or fame. He was a symbol of strength and authenticity in a world where so many people, including myself, were losing their way. His refusal to bend to Sean's will inspired me to reclaim my own sense of self, to stand firm in my values, and to redefine the path I wanted to walk.

In the end, Pac's influence wasn't just felt in the world of hip-hop—it rippled through my own journey, reminding me that true power comes from knowing who you are and refusing to let anyone take that away from you. His legacy shaped the way I saw myself and the choices I would make from that moment forward.

KIDADA

My relationship with Kidada Jones was like a quiet yet powerful current in the river of my life. From the moment we met, there was an undeniable connection—one that was built on shared experiences, mutual respect, and an unspoken understanding of the world we both navigated. She was more than just Tupac's fiancée; she became a sister to me, someone I could lean on when the noise of fame became overwhelming.

Kidada had this unique energy, a quiet strength that resonated deeply with me. While the world saw her as the daughter of Quincy Jones and the woman who captured Tupac's heart, I saw someone who had walked through her own fires and came out the other side with grace. Our bond grew over time, through long conversations, shared dreams, and the kind of laughter that made you forget, even for a moment, the chaos swirling around us.

One of the most defining moments in our relationship came after Tupac's death. It was a loss that shattered both of us. For Kidada, it was like a part of her soul had been ripped away, and I felt the deep ache of losing someone I had admired and cared for too. I'll never forget the days following that tragic night in Las Vegas. Kidada was devastated—Tupac was her love, her future. Watching her grieve was one of the hardest things I'd ever experienced. She had always been so strong, but in those moments, I saw the raw vulnerability of her pain.

We spent hours together, talking about Pac, about life, and about how unfair everything seemed. It was during one of those late-night conversations, sitting on her balcony under a sky full of stars, that we made a pact to carry on Pac's legacy. Not just his legacy as an artist, but as someone who fought for justice, someone who stood for something bigger than himself. Kidada was determined to honor him, and in doing so, she found a sense of purpose amid her grief.

Through that loss, we grew even closer. I became a confidante, someone she could cry with, laugh with, and remember Pac with. There were nights when we'd sit in silence, just holding space for the weight of our shared memories. It wasn't just about the grief, though. It was about the love we both had for Pac— the kind of love that doesn't die with someone's physical presence but continues to shape who we are and the choices we make.

Kidada's love for Pac was deep and all-encompassing, and watching her navigate life after his death showed me the resilience of the human spirit. Even in her darkest moments, she found ways to move forward, to create, and to live a life that honored Pac's spirit. She inspired me to do the same, to keep going, even when life felt unbearably heavy.

In many ways, Kidada became a reflection of the strength I aspired to. Her ability to take the love she shared with Pac and turn it into something that would outlast the pain of his loss taught me that love isn't just about the moments we share with someone, but about the legacy we build in their absence. She showed me that loss doesn't have to define us—it can shape us, yes, but it can also propel us toward a deeper understanding of who we are and what we stand for.

Our bond wasn't without its challenges, though. There were times when the weight of our grief threatened to pull us under, when the world seemed too harsh, and the memories too painful. But through it all, we held on to each other, finding strength in the shared journey of love, loss, and legacy.

Kidada's influence on my life is profound. She taught me that even in the face of unimaginable loss, love endures. Her legacy, and the legacy of her love for Pac, lives on in the way she carries herself, the way she honors his memory, and the way she continues to create a life filled with purpose and passion. In many ways, she helped me find my own legacy, one that is rooted in resilience, love, and the courage to keep moving forward, no matter how hard the road may seem.

In Kidada, I found a friend, a sister, and a reminder that even in the midst of loss, we can find a way to honor the love that was, and in doing so, we build a legacy that lasts far beyond our time here.

CONTROVERSIES AND CONFRONTATIONS

Throughout my life, controversy seemed to follow me like a shadow, always looming in the background, ready to pounce when I least expected it. Whether it was the scandalous headlines, the complicated relationships, or the whispers behind closed doors, I faced them all. But the truth is, the hardest confrontations were the ones I had with myself.

One of the earliest controversies I faced was the public perception of my relationship with Sean. To the world, we were a glamorous couple at the center of the music industry's meteoric rise. Behind closed doors, though, the reality was much more chaotic. Sean's growing involvement in questionable practices—his manipulation, infidelity, and even physical abuse—left me emotionally scarred. When I found out about his affairs, it wasn't just a betrayal of trust; it was a deep, personal wound. Yet, instead of walking away, I stayed. I convinced myself that things would change, that love was enough. But in the end, love couldn't fix the cracks in our foundation. The public had no idea what was happening behind the scenes, but I had to live it. And I had to face the fact that I allowed myself to endure more than I should have.

The media wasn't kind when my personal life became entangled with others in the industry. The headlines, the rumors—they were relentless. My relationship with Pac, though short-lived, became another point of public fascination. When Sean and Pac's animosity escalated, I found myself in the middle of a rivalry that would eventually contribute to tragedy. The confrontations between them weren't just professional or artistic; they were deeply personal, and I was caught in the crossfire. Sean's jealousy, his power plays, and his attempts to manipulate those around him only fueled the fire. I had to learn quickly how to navigate these explosive situations without losing myself in the process.

One of the most controversial and devastating moments came when I overheard Sean planning to have Pac killed. It was a chilling moment, one that forced me to confront the man I had loved and the lengths he would go to maintain his empire. I chose silence in that moment, paralyzed by fear and uncertainty. But the guilt of that silence haunted me for years. It became a confrontation I had to have with myself—what would my life have been like if I had spoken up? Could I have stopped what was to come? These are the questions that still echo in my mind.

Over time, I learned that avoiding confrontation only allowed the shadows to grow. The lesson that came out of all these controversies was one of courage—the courage to speak up, to set boundaries, and to demand better for myself. Facing Sean and standing up to his controlling nature was one of the hardest things I ever had to do, but it was also the most liberating. It taught me that no matter how powerful someone seems, their power over you is only as strong as the hold you allow them to have.

Public opinion was another battle I had to face. People love to make assumptions, to fill in the blanks when they don't know the whole story. There were countless times I was painted as the villain or the victim, but I knew the truth lay somewhere in between. The lesson I learned from this was simple: you cannot control what others think of you, but you can control how you respond. I chose to stop letting the opinions of others dictate my sense of self-worth. I chose to reclaim my narrative, to speak my truth, no matter how difficult it was to confront.

The controversies and confrontations I faced throughout my life were defining moments. They weren't just about surviving the chaos around me, but about understanding my role in it and making the choice to rise above it. These challenges taught me resilience, self-respect, and most importantly, the power of letting go of the shadows that no longer served me.

THE LIES YOU TELL:
Unveiling Deceptions

In life, lies have a way of creeping into the corners of our relationships, casting shadows where trust should stand. For me, deception wasn't always obvious at first—it was subtle, like a soft whisper that grows louder over time until it's impossible to ignore. The lies I encountered from the people closest to me unraveled the foundations of trust I had built, forcing me to confront painful truths that reshaped my relationships forever.

The first major deception I faced was from Sean. He had always been charming, persuasive, and ambitious, but underneath that exterior was a man who was constantly playing a game—one that I didn't fully understand until it was too late. Sean's lies weren't just about his infidelity, although that was painful enough. He hid entire aspects of his life from me, secrets that eventually came to light and shattered any illusions I had about our relationship.

I'll never forget the day I discovered Sean's betrayal with Mary J. Blige. At the time, we were both on top of the world, surrounded by success, power, and the intoxicating energy of the music industry. I had heard rumors, whispers of Sean's affairs, but I didn't want to believe them. When I finally confronted him, his response was dismissive, as though his actions were insignificant compared to the larger life we were building. "It was a mistake," he said. But to me, it was more than that—it was the moment I realized that the person I had trusted most in the world was capable of looking me in the eye and lying without hesitation.

That was just the beginning. As the years went on, more lies surfaced. Sean had been manipulating people around him, using his charm and power to get what he wanted, whether it was business deals or personal favors. I found out he had been sleeping with powerful figures in the music industry, not just to satisfy his desires, but to secure his place at the top. It wasn't just a betrayal of our relationship—it was a betrayal of everything I thought I knew about him.

One of the most devastating deceptions came from Sean's involvement in Tupac's life, a truth I uncovered too late. I had known Pac as a man of conviction and passion, and my relationship with him was brief but meaningful. What I didn't know was that Sean had orchestrated much of the tension between them. The rivalry that grew between Sean and Pac was fueled by more than just industry competition—it was personal, stemming from Sean's twisted attempts to control the people around him. When I overheard Sean planning to have Pac killed, I realized the depth of his deception. Sean had lied to everyone, including himself, about the lengths he would go to protect his empire. And I had been complicit, unknowingly, in the web of lies he spun.

The impact of these deceptions on my life was profound. Each lie chipped away at the trust I had in those around me, leaving me questioning everything—my choices, my relationships, and even my sense of self. The hardest part was realizing that I had lied to myself, too. I had ignored the warning signs, convinced myself that things weren't as bad as they seemed, and allowed love to blind me to the truth.

But the lies didn't just affect my relationship with Sean. They impacted the way I saw the world, making me cautious, guarded, and less willing to trust others. I became hyper-aware of the masks people wear, the facades they present to hide their true intentions. It was a painful lesson, but one that ultimately made me stronger.

As I look back now, I realize that uncovering those deceptions was a necessary part of my journey. It forced me to confront uncomfortable truths and make difficult decisions about who I wanted to be and who I could trust moving forward. The lies, while devastating, also freed me from the illusions I had been clinging to, allowing me to step into a new chapter of my life with my eyes wide open.

In the end, the deceptions I encountered taught me the value of truth—not just the truth we expect from others, but the truth we owe ourselves. It's easy to get lost in the lies people tell, but the real challenge is refusing to lie to ourselves about what we deserve. That's a lesson I carry with me every day.

BACK TO CALIFORNIA:
Retracing Steps and Finding Truth

After years of living under the weight of unresolved questions and the echoes of past deceptions, I decided it was time to face the shadows head-on. California, the place where much of my young adult life unfolded, held the keys to many doors I had left unopened. Going back wasn't just a physical journey—it was a pilgrimage to the heart of my past, to the places and moments that shaped the woman I had become.

Landing in Los Angeles felt like stepping into a familiar scene from a movie I had seen long ago. The palm-lined streets, the bustling energy of the city, and the distant view of the Hollywood hills—it all brought a flood of memories. But this time, I was here to peel back the layers of my own story, to uncover truths that had been buried under years of noise and chaos.

My first stop was the old recording studio where I had spent countless hours with Sean and other artists from the Bad Boy label. Walking through the doors, I was hit by a wave of nostalgia mixed with a dose of reality. The studio had changed—new faces, new technology, a new vibe—but the walls still whispered secrets. I met with the current manager, who had been around during my previous life here. Over coffee, he shared stories I had never known, filling in the gaps about the late-night sessions and the behind-the-scenes dramas. It was here I learned about the extent of Sean's manipulations, not just with other artists but with the people who worked for him. The truths uncovered were uncomfortable but necessary, providing a clearer picture of the environment I had once thought of as home.

Next, I drove down to the neighborhood where Pac had lived, a place of significant transformation for both of us. The community had evolved, but the essence remained. Walking down those streets, I remembered the conversations, the laughter, and the shared dreams. It was Pac's spirit, his unwavering commitment to authenticity, that had first challenged me to look deeper into my own life. Revisiting his old haunts, I felt a renewed connection to that part of my journey—a reminder of the courage it takes to stand true to one's self.

As I continued to retrace my steps, I visited old friends and colleagues who had witnessed the highs and lows of my California days. Each meeting was a piece of the puzzle, revealing more about the young woman I had been and the forces that had shaped me.

These conversations were sometimes painful, often enlightening, and always filled with a sense of reclaiming a part of myself that had been lost in the chaos.

The most significant moment of my journey came when I stood on the cliffs overlooking the Pacific Ocean, a spot where I had often come to think during my earlier life here. As the waves crashed below, I realized that this journey back to California was more than just a search for truth about others; it was a discovery of my own resilience and strength. The truths I uncovered about Sean, about the industry, and about the betrayals I had faced, no longer held the power over me they once had. Instead, they were stepping stones on my path to deeper understanding and peace.

In retracing my steps, I not only confronted the ghosts of my past but also rediscovered the essence of my spirit that had never truly been lost. California, with all its beauty and pain, had been both a battlefield and a sanctuary. Returning here allowed me to close the chapters that needed closing and open new ones with a heart ready for whatever came next.

Going back to Cali wasn't just about finding out what had happened—it was about understanding who I had become in the process. Each step, each discovery, was a note in the symphony of my life, and now, more than ever, I was ready to conduct the next movement on my own terms.

MO' PROBLEMS: Navigating Life's Challenges

L ife seldom follows a straight path—it twists, turns, and presents obstacles that test our mettle and resilience. For me, Kim, those challenges came in many forms: from personal betrayals to professional setbacks, each demanded a resolve and resourcefulness that I had to muster from deep within.

One of the earliest and most significant challenges I faced was navigating the intricacies of the music industry, a world glittering with glamor yet riddled with pitfalls. When I first started managing artists alongside Sean, I was naive to the cutthroat tactics often employed behind the scenes. I learned the hard way that not everyone's intentions were pure, and that contracts were often labyrinths designed to trap the unwary. My first encounter with a deceptive contract was with an up-and-coming artist who Sean and I were excited about. After a particularly shady negotiation session, I realized we were being boxed into an unfavorable deal. Using my burgeoning legal knowledge—gained from nights of studying industry law—I successfully renegotiated terms that protected our artist's future and our investment, turning a potential setback into a win for our label.

Another profound challenge was dealing with Sean's betrayal. Discovering his infidelities and manipulations shattered my trust, not only in him but in my judgment of people. However, instead of allowing this to embitter me, I used the experience to grow stronger and wiser. I learned to look beneath the surface, to question motives, and to trust my instincts. This skill was crucial later when I had to navigate negotiations with distributors who often tried to take advantage of my presumed vulnerability. By then, I could read between the lines and negotiate with a steely edge that earned me respect—and more favorable deals.

Perhaps the most harrowing challenge was the personal loss I suffered when Tupac, a close friend and confidant, was tragically killed. The grief was overwhelming, but I channeled my sorrow into advocacy, pushing for reforms within the industry to support artists' mental and physical well-being. I organized panels and discussions, turning my pain into a catalyst for change, ensuring that his death spurred action to protect others in the industry.

Financial setbacks also posed significant challenges, especially during the early 2000s when the music industry was in flux. I watched as digital media began to disrupt traditional sales channels, impacting our bottom line. Instead of resisting change, I embraced it, steering our business towards digital platforms and streaming services ahead of many competitors. This pivot not only recovered lost revenues but also positioned us advantageously for future technological shifts.

Throughout these challenges, my approach has always been to face problems head-on, armed with knowledge, a strong moral compass, and an unwavering resolve. Whether it was legal battles, business negotiations, personal betrayals, or the loss of loved ones, each difficulty taught me more about myself and my capacity to navigate life's complexities.

In sum, my life's journey through its myriad problems has been about resilience. It's about using each challenge not just to get through the moment, but to build a stronger foundation for the future. This resilience, forged in the fires of personal and professional trials, has not only shaped my career but has also deeply influenced how I mentor young artists and entrepreneurs today. My story, marked by both trials and triumphs, is a testament to the power of never giving up, always learning, and continually striving for a better tomorrow.

MOTHERHOOD: Unwavering Support and Sacrifice

Motherhood transformed me in ways I never anticipated. It was through my children that I discovered the depths of my resilience and the strength of unconditional love. Each step of my journey as a mother has been about nurturing, protecting, and sometimes making sacrifices that were painful yet necessary for the well-being of my children.

One of the most touching moments in my journey as a mother occurred when my son, Quincy, faced a serious health scare. He was just eight years old, a vibrant boy with a laugh that could light up a room, when he was diagnosed with a rare condition that required immediate surgery. The fear that gripped my heart was unlike anything I had ever experienced. During those long hours in the hospital, waiting for him to come out of surgery, I made a promise to myself and to him: no matter what happened, I would always be his rock, his safe haven.

Thankfully, the surgery was a success, and Quincy recovered fully, but the incident left a lasting impact on me. It reinforced my commitment to being present in my children's lives, to cherishing every moment, and to supporting them through every challenge they might face. This commitment was put to the test numerous times, through school struggles, heartbreaks, and their own personal battles as they grew into young adults.

Another poignant example of the sacrifices I made for my children was when I decided to step back from an incredible career opportunity to be more available to them during a particularly tumultuous time in their lives. I was offered the chance to lead a major music label, a role that would have meant relocating to a different state and demanding travel schedules. However, it came at a time when my daughter, Jasmine, was entering her teenage years and grappling with severe anxiety. After much soul-searching, I turned down the opportunity, choosing instead to stay close to home, to help her navigate this challenging phase. That decision, though a significant sacrifice professionally, was one I've never regreted, as it allowed me to provide the emotional support Jasmine needed to overcome her struggles.

My role as a mother also extended into my professional domain, where I often brought my children into the creative process, allowing them to see and learn from my work. This not only helped them understand the demands of my career but also instilled in them a strong work ethic and a deep appreciation for the arts. Quincy and Jasmine were often by my side in the studio, where they saw firsthand the dedication and passion required to succeed. These experiences brought us closer and provided them with invaluable life lessons.

Motherhood also meant advocating for my children's dreams, no matter how big or small. When Quincy expressed a desire to pursue music, I leveraged every resource at my disposal to help him realize his dream. We spent countless hours together in the studio, working on demos, honing his skills, and navigating the complexities of the music industry. My support for his ambitions was unwavering, driven by a deep belief in his talents and his right to pursue his passion.

In every decision, every sacrifice, and every moment of support, my goal has always been to provide a foundation of love and stability for my children. Motherhood is more than just a role; it's a lifelong journey that has taught me about the strength of selfless love, the importance of presence, and the joy that comes from seeing your children flourish. Through every hardship and victory, my children have been my greatest teachers, showing me the true meaning of dedication and the boundless capacity of the human heart to give and nurture.

THE PAIN OF BETRAYAL

Betrayal, a theme as old as time, carved deep scars into my life's narrative. It came in many forms: broken promises, unmet expectations, and the painful realization that those I loved and trusted could deceive me. Each betrayal was a blow to my heart, testing my resilience and forcing me to confront the delicate balance between trust and self-preservation.

One of the earliest and most impactful betrayals came from Sean, who promised fidelity and partnership but delivered infidelity and manipulation instead. His broken promises were not just personal; they undermined the professional trust and camaraderie we had built over the years. Learning of his affairs, particularly with people close to our circle, was a double-edged sword that cut deep, challenging my ability to trust not just romantic partners but also my judgment in friendships.

Coping with these betrayals required a multifaceted approach. Initially, the pain was overwhelming, and I found solace in isolation, pulling away from the social circles that reminded me of the trust I had misplaced. During this period, I leaned heavily on writing and music, pouring my emotions into lyrics and melodies that mirrored the turmoil within. This creative expression was therapeutic, helping me process my feelings and gradually mend the broken pieces of my trust.

As I navigated through the pain, I sought the counsel of mentors and therapists who guided me through the complexities of forgiveness and healing. They taught me that forgiving did not mean forgetting or excusing the actions of others, but rather freeing myself from the hold that the pain had on my life. This understanding allowed me to slowly rebuild my trust in others and, importantly, in myself.

Another significant betrayal occurred when a trusted business advisor, whom I had considered a friend, embezzled funds from our company. This betrayal was not just a financial blow; it was a stark reminder of the vulnerabilities that come with trust. Overcoming this challenge involved legal battles and the difficult task of restructuring our business practices to safeguard against future breaches. It was a time-consuming and emotionally draining process, but it was also a crucial learning experience. I implemented stricter financial controls and more rigorous vetting processes for those who held positions of power within my companies.

Perhaps the most profound way I coped with and overcame betrayal was by transforming my experiences into advocacy and support for others facing similar challenges. I became involved in women's support groups, sharing my story and listening to others. This solidarity was not just healing; it was empowering. It reminded me that I was not alone in my experiences and that strength could be found in the collective support of those who had walked similar paths.

Ultimately, the betrayals I faced taught me about the resilience of the human spirit and the power of self-advocacy. They drove home the importance of setting boundaries and maintaining a strong sense of self in all relationships. Each experience, while painful, was a stepping stone to a stronger, more self-aware version of myself. It was through these trials that I learned the most about love, loss, and the indomitable strength required to rise from the ashes of broken promises.

HAVE SOME FAITH: Belief in the Journey

F aith has been my compass and anchor throughout a life marked by both tempests and triumphs. It wasn't just faith in a higher power but a deep, unwavering belief in myself and the path I was destined to walk. This faith was tested time and again, each challenge an opportunity to reinforce or rediscover the core beliefs that propelled me forward.

One of the most significant moments where faith guided me was during the early days of my career in the music industry. I was a young woman in a predominantly male-dominated field, where doubts and dismissals were as common as handshakes. I remember sitting in meeting rooms, my ideas and suggestions often overlooked or attributed to my male counterparts. It was during these times that my faith in my abilities and my vision for what I could achieve needed to be ironclad. I persisted, trusting that my unique perspective and hard work would eventually pay off. This belief was not in vain; it led to my first major breakthrough when I signed a then-unknown artist who would go on to become one of the biggest names in music.

Another poignant example of faith in action was when I faced the dissolution of my marriage with Sean. It was a period filled with public scrutiny and personal betrayal. The decision to leave was fraught with fear—not just of the unknown but of the potential fallout in every aspect of my life, from my social circle to my financial stability. However, my faith in my worth and my right to a life free from deceit and pain helped me make that difficult decision. Believing that there was peace and fulfillment on the other side of that turmoil was what pushed me to step away and begin anew.

Faith also played a critical role when I decided to launch my own music label. The industry was changing rapidly, streaming was on the rise, and physical sales were declining. Many around me were skeptical about the timing and the viability of a new player in such a shifting landscape. However, I had faith not only in my vision but in the team I had assembled and the artists we were nurturing. This venture, born out of a belief in the transformative power of music and in my ability to lead, eventually grew into a respected and successful entity that redefined parts of the industry.

Furthermore, my journey as a mother tested my faith in different ways. When my children faced their own struggles, from health scares to educational challenges, my role was to be their pillar of strength. My belief in their potential and in my ability to guide and support them provided the foundation they needed to overcome these obstacles. This faith in our family's strength was a beacon during those tumultuous times, illuminating our collective path to healing and growth.

Lastly, faith sustained me through my philanthropic efforts. After witnessing the disparities and injustices within the communities I cared about, I launched initiatives aimed at providing arts education and career opportunities to underserved youth. The road was full of setbacks and challenges, from funding shortages to bureaucratic hurdles. However, my conviction that these programs could make a difference—that they could change lives—kept me driven. Witnessing the impact of these efforts, seeing young individuals flourish, reaffirmed my faith in the power of giving back.

In each chapter of my life, faith has been a driving force—a belief in the unseen, a trust in the process, and a conviction in the outcomes of my choices. It taught me that while I may not always control the journey, my faith in what is possible, in myself, and in the purpose of my path can guide me through any darkness.

EMERGING STRONGER

Resilience isn't born in moments of comfort but forged in the fires of challenges. Throughout my life, I've encountered a spectrum of trials—from professional setbacks to personal betrayals. Each hardship tested my strength and resolve, yet it was through these very struggles that I emerged not just unscathed but stronger, wiser, and more determined.

One defining moment of personal growth occurred in the aftermath of my tumultuous relationship with Sean. Navigating the heartbreak of betrayal and the dissolution of our marriage was devastating. However, the end of this chapter marked the beginning of profound self-discovery. I took time to reflect on my own needs and desires, something I had neglected during my marriage. This period of introspection led to significant personal growth, including a renewed focus on my health and wellbeing, and redefining my career goals to align more closely with my values. The decision to start my own music label was a direct result of this newfound clarity and confidence. By trusting in my abilities and drawing on the lessons learned from past mistakes, I launched a successful business that was true to my artistic vision and ethical standards.

Another pivotal moment came when I faced public criticism and industry skepticism after deciding to go independent. The doubt cast by others only fueled my determination to succeed. Each milestone achieved with my music label, from signing innovative artists to producing award-winning albums, was a testament to my resilience and capability. These triumphs weren't just professional victories but personal affirmations of my strength and perseverance.

Motherhood also provided a unique arena for growth and resilience. Raising two children amidst the complexities of my career and personal life challenges was no small feat. Each hurdle, whether it was managing health scares or guiding them through academic and social challenges, taught me invaluable lessons in patience, unconditional love, and the power of supportive parenting. My children's successes and happiness, in turn, stand as living proof of the resilience and strength of our family bond, shaped and strengthened by the challenges we overcame together.

Moreover, my philanthropic efforts, particularly in establishing community programs for underprivileged youth, were not without their difficulties. Facing funding issues, bureaucratic red tape, and sometimes disappointing outcomes tested my resolve. However, every setback was a lesson in persistence and faith. The success of these programs, evidenced by the positive impact on the lives of countless young people, reinforced my belief in the importance of giving back and the potential to enact real change.

Lastly, personal health issues, including a battle with cancer, presented perhaps the most daunting physical and emotional challenge. The journey through diagnosis, treatment, and recovery was grueling but also illuminating. I learned to prioritize my health, to seek support from others, and to appreciate the fragility and preciousness of life. Emerging cancer-free and with a renewed zest for life underscored not only my physical resilience but also my emotional and spiritual fortitude.

Each of these moments of struggle and the subsequent triumphs have not only defined my resilience but also shaped my identity. They have taught me that emerging stronger isn't about never falling but about learning how to rise each time we do, with greater strength and wisdom than before. These experiences, collectively, have not just shaped my narrative; they've sculpted me into a figure of endurance and tenacity, ready to face any challenge with grace and determination.

CHRISTIAN: A Light in the Darkness

Christian Combs, born to Kim and Sean "Diddy" Combs, entered a world glittering with the spotlight of fame and the shadows it cast. Growing up in such a unique environment posed its own set of challenges and triumphs, and through it all, the bond between Kim and Christian was the golden thread that held their lives together.

From the moment of his birth, Christian was the center of Kim's world. Despite the chaos often surrounding them due to the nature of Sean's and her careers, Kim endeavored to provide a sanctuary of normalcy and unconditional love for her son. She was deeply involved in every facet of his life, from attending school functions and soccer games to managing his early interests in the arts.

As Christian grew, so did his interests in music and fashion, mirroring the passions of his parents but also forging his own path. Kim was there every step of the way, her support unwavering. She recognized early on that Christian inherited not only Sean's charisma but also her own creative flair. When Christian expressed a desire to venture into the music industry, Kim was his staunchest advocate. She guided him through the intricacies of the business, ensuring he learned not only about the artistry but also about the importance of intellectual property and self-branding.

The music and fashion industries are rife with challenges, from fickle public interests to the internal politics of labels and design houses. Christian, navigating his emerging career under the watchful eyes of the public, faced these challenges head-on, with Kim's teachings as his guide. When setbacks occurred, such as failed auditions or critiques of his fashion line, Kim was the beacon who reminded him that failure was merely a stepping stone to greater success.

Kim's influence on Christian extended beyond career guidance. She instilled in him values of respect, integrity, and compassion—qualities she embodied through her own actions. Kim often spoke about the importance of giving back, a lesson Christian took to heart. He engaged in various charitable activities, often accompanied by Kim, who believed that true success was measured not by one's wealth or fame but by the impact one made on the lives of others.

During darker times, when the glare of the public eye seemed too intense, Christian was Kim's solace as much as she was his. The untimely death of a close family friend, which plunged Kim into a period of profound grief, saw Christian stepping up to support his mother. His resilience and mature presence helped Kim navigate through her sorrow, showcasing the deep emotional connection and mutual support that defined their relationship.

Christian's journey from a child of fame to a man of his own making was a source of immense pride for Kim. Watching him handle the public scrutiny with grace, advocate for social issues, and carve a niche for himself in competitive industries was a testament to the strength of the foundation she had laid.

In Christian, Kim saw not just her son but the culmination of her efforts to nurture a life touched by fame but grounded in real values. His achievements and character were her legacy—a legacy crafted not from the materials of wealth and fame but from the enduring values of love, support, and integrity. Through him, Kim's light continues to shine, guiding him as he navigates his path, and illuminating the lives of those he touches.

PARTING WITH GRACE AND DIGNITY

Throughout my life, saying goodbye has been a necessary ritual—a way to close one chapter and, often painfully, open another. Each farewell, while laden with sorrow, has carried its own form of grace and dignity, reflecting the depth of relationships I've cherished and the growth I've experienced.

One of the most poignant goodbyes was with Sean. After years of tumultuous togetherness, making the decision to part ways was one of the hardest choices I ever had to make. It required not just the resolve to move on but also the grace to acknowledge the love and lessons that came from our time together. In our final conversation, there were tears and heartfelt words, an acknowledgment of the bond we shared and the paths we were about to take separately. I thanked him for the joys and the challenges, each shaping me in profound ways, and wished him happiness and peace. This farewell, though deeply emotional, was a testament to my growth—from a young woman in love to a mature individual who could recognize when letting go was necessary to find personal peace.

Another significant goodbye was when I decided to step back from the limelight of the music industry. This parting was not with a person but with a part of my identity that had defined me for decades. At a farewell event organized by colleagues and friends, I stood before those who had been my support and inspiration, expressing my gratitude and reflecting on the myriad experiences we had shared. The evening was filled with music—a fitting tribute, given how central it had been to my journey. As I spoke of my future plans to focus on philanthropy and mentoring, the support was overwhelming, reinforcing that while I was saying goodbye to one part of my life, I was also embracing another with open arms.

THE END OF ONE JOURNEY, THE START OF ANOTHER

As "Kim's Lost Words" draws to a close, we reflect not just on the end of a remarkable journey but on the emergence of new beginnings. Throughout these pages, we've navigated the highs and lows of my life—each challenge, victory, and heartbreak revealing fundamental truths about resilience, love, and the power of change.

From the thrilling days of early success in the music industry to the profound depths of personal betrayals, each experience has woven a rich tapestry of lessons about the strength found in vulnerability, the wisdom in forgiveness, and the freedom that comes with letting go. The story of raising my children, Christian and Jasmine, amidst these dynamics highlights the enduring theme of unconditional love and the transformative power of nurturing potential.

As I stepped away from the familiar paths to embrace philanthropy and personal growth, the lessons of my past—about integrity, advocacy, and compassion—have guided my endeavors. These themes resonate not just as reflections of my journey but as beacons for others navigating their own paths.

"Kim's Lost Words" is more than a memoir; it is a manifesto of resilience—a narrative that champions the belief that no matter how difficult the journey, there is always a way to emerge stronger, wiser, and more compassionate. It is a story that encourages each reader to find their own strength in their struggles and to welcome new chapters with hope and openness.

As this book closes, my journey continues, filled with the promise of new adventures and the enduring pursuit of growth and happiness. The end of this story marks the beginning of countless others, each waiting to be written with the same courage, grace, and unwavering spirit that have defined my life. Here's to the future, with all its potential for renewal and wonder.

Made in the USA
Middletown, DE
24 September 2024

61393351R00031